Black Cart

Black Cart

Jim Carruth

FREIGHT BOOKS

First published 2017

Freight Books
49–53 Virginia Street
Glasgow, G1 1TS
www.freightbooks.co.uk

ISBN 978-1-911332-35-0

Typeset by Freight in Plantin
Printed and bound by Bell and Bain, Glasgow

the publisher acknowledges investment from
Creative Scotland toward the publication of this book

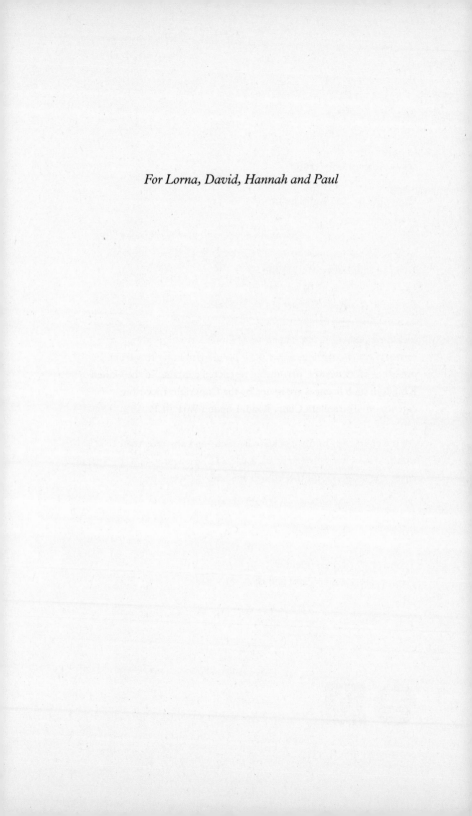

For Lorna, David, Hannah and Paul

Contents

III Inheritance

Homecoming

O ubi campi!
          Virgil

Homecoming

As I drive, you dream on in the back seat
unaware that motorways have narrowed to lanes,
safe in the guiltless sleep only children manage.
My thoughts are with what is forgotten.
Breeds and crosses have become
cows and sheep in nursery books.
Strains of rye-grass are broad-brushed fields:
greens and yellows merged at speed.

I want to learn again the art of careful detail.
A wood pigeon's soft calling
from Scots pines on Harelaw,
a fox on the skyline returning home,
an early morning tractor ploughing for barley.
I smell the damson above the diesel,
I taste the earth.
By the time we cross over the Locher Bridge
my feet on the pedals are paddling in frog spawn.
So easily it slips between the toes.

Turning the final corner
I picture my welcome:
the bark the collie gives a stranger;
the slow burn of recognition
in a wrinkled face; and my words,
faltering and uncertain,
like the first unsteady steps of an Ayrshire calf
staggering towards her mother
with a hunger new born.

Harelaw

Searchlight

A toddler double-wrapped in heavy woollens,
wedged snug in the open mouth of a ten gallon can,

I'd watch my parents work down the stalls of Ayrshires,
drawing off milk along the cobbled byre.

Over hunched shoulders they'd check on me,
high up in my watchtower in that hall of shadows,

before bending again to attach the next machine,
and the next, till the far end swallowed them in its dark,

leaving me for a cluster's regular heartbeat
with nothing but cattle bellows, the rattle of chains.

I look for them still, listen for their returning voices;
I will them back into the light.

Barnbeth

The Burns Competition

I tried to practise
long weekday nights towards his birthday
but the words wouldn't fit in my mouth.
I stuck my tongue out at the bathroom mirror,
checked for the straying of molars
but found no obvious physical deformity.
My mother tried to help.
Her voice was natural and unforced,
still striding behind the plough
of her own father,
sure-footed on the soft curve
of Ayrshire soil.

Saturdays would find me at the back
of the hen hutch playing catch
but dropping more and more
of her fragile bantam eggs,
before running in to watch
The Flashing Blade,
Belle and Sebastian,
Robinson Crusoe,
their languages buried under
clumsily dubbed English.

On the day of the competition
despite the coaching
and the strip of limp tartan
pinned to my shirt,
the words in my hand
were as lifeless as Maggie's tail
while the boy in our class from Leicester
was modulating his voice
in exaggerated accents,
contorting his face in false passion,

Barcraig

gesticulating his way
through an overblown performance,
taking the piss,
winning by a country mile.

Educating the Farm Boy

It came

as no surprise to me

43 pages from the end of the second part

of *The Ingenious Gentleman Don Quixote of La Mancha,*

Edith Grossman's translation of the Miguel de Cervantes classic,

that the eponymous knight's increasing madness

of quests and giants should reach its climax

with his decision to become

a farmer of

sheep.

Tapestry

Up late
while the last of the sticks
crackled on the fire,
I'd watch my mother

hold the wool end
to her mouth
licking a point
pushing it through an eye of silver.

Caught in the glow,
her face hovered
above the wooden frame.
With a kingfisher dive

the needle disappeared and surfaced
pulling out rainbows
time and again
double back and cut.

Her hands rough and calloused
hacked deep with shadow
thumbnail snecked black
crushed by a chain in the bull pen.

During the day these hands
held sodden bales
(strings sliced deep into skin);
carried calves minutes old

slippery as eels;
gripped frozen milk pails;
graiped silage into troughs;
dried small tears;

dressed four of us for school;
wrenched green shaws
from ribbed carrots;
chopped potatoes and leeks

that simmered for hours
for one of those thick sweet soups
we could taste
as we stepped off the bus.

The hands
my daughter watches today
threading colours
through a new canvas.

8

Into the Blue

It was more than the pain of its recoil,
the purple flourish of a shoulder bruise
that took several weeks to leave my body;
more than their coarse laughter or tardy advice
that I should have held it firm like a man
or my worry throughout this rite of passage;
my struggle to lift the double barrel
and its heavy weight to almost horizontal.

My father's success with it filled our pantry
but I never went hunting with him to the woods.
Instead I stood barefoot on a cold stone floor
and faced the lifeless works in his gallery:
vermilion daubed across wing and breast,
pheasant and mallard hung like roosting bats;
lifeless hares flopped on a shelf:
away from the field, no longer themselves.

Now close to seventy he argues to keep his licence
as though the gun is a crucial part of him:
man-made like the plastic knee and hip
that prevent him from shooting on the hill.
Nobody else will use it; when he dies it will go.
On that day decades ago I was supposed
to knock an old soup can off the fence post
but winged a cloud and brought down the sky.

Bridgepark

Drowning Kittens

Drowning kittens is cruel, my father says as he shows me
the new litter, plucked from a warm hollow in the bales,
brought from that sanctuary in the barn into sunlight.

Their fur captures patches from the visiting tom. Their eyes
are the smallest I've ever seen, our heads the size of clouds.
But you know we can't keep them. He watches my face.
Too many cats already and not enough food to go round.

I look down to the burn, think of the newborn huddled
in a hessian sack closed tight at the top with bale strings,
imagine them, as he must, spluttering in the rushing dark.
I choke on their life's final seconds, turn back to my father.

Two kittens lie cradled broken-necked across his left hand;
the last, chapped eyes wide open against a roughcast wall.

Mare

Landscape with the Fall of Icarus
after Brueghel

No, he hadn't heard a thing
what with being up before dawn
getting the old horse watered and fed
checking on the shepherd
after his night in the fields,
that boy – head always in the clouds
then harnessing up the mare
and all day struggling
with the heavy plough
to keep the horse going
to keep the furrows even
to finish the field before nightfall
with the weather on the change
and the wind picking up
when would he ever
have had time to stop
to listen for a flurry
of wings, a solitary far-off splash
and to recognise it
as anything more than a gull.

The Trouble with Ploughing

The trouble with ploughing is
 it rarely offers itself up to sought for perfection
  even in the hands of the experienced and skilled
   with the most modern plough and a willing field.

The trouble with ploughing is
 you are never truly in control of the journey
  the ever changing angle of slope and rain
   working against the quest for a flawless line.

The trouble with ploughing is
 too soon you are forced to face your mistakes
  the perspective of the return journey reveals
   all that could have been and now too late to sort.

The trouble with ploughing is
 the finished field is a testament to your failings
  all winter it will haunt you like a ruined canvas
   and you'll long for it to be masked in deep snow.

The trouble with ploughing is
 you are drawn back to the same field each year
  it will not let you go and is never any easier
   for the soil is shallower, the old blade blunter.

The trouble with ploughing is
 that so poor was I at the tractor driving basics
  hapless with the harrow, scraper and trailer
   I was never given a chance to try one furrow.

12

The Moleman's Apprentice

surfaced
one Friday night
at the village hall
and asked her to dance,
leading the way
through the crowded floor, parting
couples who closed
in tight
behind them. All evening
she stared
into his small eyes,
felt his first beard
soft-furred
on her face;
but that's not
what she remembers,
nor his dirty long nails,
his spade-hands, his proud
boasting that in a first week
measured in pelts
he had plucked the dead
from their dark: instead,
it was near the end –
some joker flicked
a switch and cut
the power:
his shudder and scream
as the night snapped shut.

Calves

Barn Dance

Counting down to Christmas,
neighbours gather at night
sitting in line to receive gifts

dropped on expectant laps –
solid weight, warm tremor,
limp swing of a wattled neck.

Veterans quick-flick a rhythm,
talk of difficult calvings,
the scarcity of good hay.

It's in the wrist action:
Don't tug – you'll bruise the meat.
The barn explodes

feathers and defecation,
spasms of the new dead;
one corpse catapults across the floor.

This splay-toed pogo
of a half-mohican
trails the broken arc of a fan.

It's the dance of a daftie
one cousin quips.
Others stay quiet

watching the bird falter,
flop down to an end planned
since the shell's first crack.

Fighting the Beast

The herd in the Meadow
stand up to their hocks in muck
gorging themselves on our daily gift:
forked silage reeking

of warmer days. Icy peat water surges
from its lair on the moor
to devour the shallow burn,
branches tangled in its earth-soiled hide.

We find a heifer lying half-submerged.
The rope is fetched, harnessed and taut –
the tractor labouring to pluck a life from the flood.

The torrent clawing at our feet
wrenches away the river's edge,
drowns the growl of a collie,
our curses, the cow's hoarse bellow. Slithering

from futile toe-holds on the slope,
we become the colour of the bank
sapped by sleet-driven hours in the heavy clay,
shoving on, aching shoulders against pin bone,
sharing cold tremors of the frightened cow.

Her matted tail flicks against raw cheeks.
Our white teeth grit tighter through the murk
while the straining tractor's headlights
catch small jewelled eyes on higher ground.
It shudders forward – the beast gives up its prey.

The Field

Afterwards, my father walked to the Mare:
one of the far fields on the hill of Barcraig
crowned by a crescent of elder and chestnut.

He listened to the calls of curlew and peewit,
remembered shafts of light and summer days,
recognised the breeze as an endless breath

over rough acres fenced but not fully tamed:
large clumps of whin, thistles, rye grass,
a heart of marsh reeds sloping to the burn.

He looked to Muirshiel's dark and brackened hills
round to the hard-won grazing of the Law,
and further to the creep of city high-rise.

He raised one strong arm across his body
then, with the grace of a sower's wide arc,
scattered his father to the wind.

Hilltop

Making a Mark

All morning spent wrestling calves in the pen
to bring each in turn to where my father waits
ready with his heavy pliers and a jar of black tar.
In his head he stores the markings of each child
and know its mother, father, previous generations.

So with this in mind and with a printer's care
he sets out precisely a row of letters and numbers
like teeth along the open mouth of the silver pliers;
the order that makes every identity unique
their relationship to the herd – breeding is all.

I press the writhing body of the young beast
against the rails of the gate in a corner;
present the head clenched, tilted and still.
Avoiding all ridges and blood vessels
we ensure the text is central to the ear.

Then the crunch of the pliers against the lobe.
The calf rears up, its young body convulses,
but committed to the cause I grip on tight
as my father tars with care the puncture holes,
keen to capture for life the clarity of the line.

Wellpark

Hunger of the Muse

From a field this small, from a soil thin and poor
from the worst that the unreliable seasons bring

from the hard toil that never reaps its full reward
from the heartbreak of harvests lost to the land

from all those that will never reach full height
but broken by the wind as their awns sing out

from each unripe ear – these small hard kernels
today you will bake for me the sweetest bread.

Bethlem
'after years addicted to Poetical prosing'
Dr Fenwick Skrimshire (anent John Clare)

Sae is it gift or ailin
tae wend yer way atween dowie and raving,
twa poles o madness placed heich abune yer heid?
Embrace thaim baith as brithers.

Kept ahint those lockit doors I ken tae weel
ye will swing frae months o leid drooth,
lang mirk days when ye cannae speik,
tae endless oors o pynefu yowl,
deleerit, clawin at yer blankets
nakit an shackled, fauchelt yet strang.

Wi lollin tongue an glaikit gawk
yer een lik wanderin yowes,
yer boady thrawn and taut,
yer gob boakin up yer wird hoard.

Nae doot they will try tae sain ye,
pit the branks oan yer ill urges,
scour ye o yer black gaw,
fix yer aff kilter muids,
bluid ye o yer spasms –
shak ye frae yer dwaum.

Haud oan ticht tae yer helter-skelter raverie
Niver let thaim tame yer wit in tongues
nor tether yer dementit makar's thochts
an souse foriver yer ain sae sweet burdsang.

The Word

i
Through showers and sun
Thought and passion

ii
Beneath the bellow of a bull
Passion and the voice

iii
Bleating from the byre
Voice forming sound

iv
Shepherd's sharp whistle
Sound shaping word

v
Wing beat in a skein
Word on a line

vi
Furrow left in a field
Line on a page

vii
Each fleece in the flock
Page and chapter

viii
Beside a piglet, a sow
Chapter and the book

ix
As barley to a combine
Book and the reader

x
Hungry calf at the pail
Reader and the word

The Man Who Wanted to Hug Cows

On his good days, he'd walk out from the village,
lose himself in country lanes, drawing blood from brambles
or stare across fields mumbling to himself.
They called him professor, though no one knew his past;
the postman brought rumours of separation and breakdown.

When first asked, farmers said no.
One relented, pointing him to a quiet Friesian.
Seemed harmless enough he told his neighbour later
but he watched him closely from the gate that first time,
uneasy at the nervousness of the stranger.

Left in peace, for long afternoons
he'd cling around folds of the heifer's neck;
whisper an echo in the beast's dark ear,
her big eyes and soft rough muzzle would turn to him.
Slow-motion slavers and heavy breath fell across his face.

To those who listen the farmer's wife still recalls
finding him asleep in the grass – a smile within the herd;
his head resting on thick-haired warmth,
lulled by the rise and fall of maternal ribs,
the beat of a larger heart.

Isaiah Turner

Our talk turns again
to the last year of his life

how we boys found him
a week after harvest end

on his knees in the set aside
beyond Smith's barley field.

Half hidden by the weeds,
he tore at his own clothes

clawed at the dry soil,
ranted at the crows.

We laughed at him
in the fallow ground

called him a fool –
the old farmer

named as a prophet
who quoted the psalms

foretold the giving up
of our father's land.

Then we took it further
torched the stubble

lost his message
in thick black smoke.

Far Field

i
Because he knows, has always known
that a time will come in the near future
when he will have no say in the matter,
will not decide the date or time of departure
but be taken from here silent or screaming,
today he commands the collie to stay home
and one more time makes this journey of choice
leaving the farm for a couple of hours,
setting off from behind the old byre,
walking over the hill to the far field,
spending time away from the needs
of family and herd.

ii
When he gets there the field will welcome him,
its gate open for that is how he leaves it
for anyone who'd take the time to travel here,
find as he does a space for thought,
safe for a moment in its heart,
the rough ground by the whins.
He disturbs a flurried brace of pheasants
then stands awhile, watching his childhood
and all the years since rise like the smoke
from the valley to drift in the wind.
However much he wants to
he cannot shake the hands
of all those loved, buried or burned.

iii
He searches for fragments and clues
and finds them in the marks he's left on this land,
cultivated grasses, fence and dyke;
the dry stane wall built up and fallen down
and raised again throughout his life.
He marks his herd, stamped through generations,
his decisions on their breeding, his choice
of bloodlines. He marks his family, his children
inheriting his weak heart, his values.
He marks himself, branded
from a lifetime on the hill.

iv
Does his life echo others in the valley,
their days sliced through with tarmacadam?
How many down there have never found their fit
and place? For them he offers up a prayer,
a promise of belonging. He offers up this field
but does not sense a bond with the valley and beyond,
content to mark them like members of his herd.
All he feels is a greater pain, a loss
that he cannot name or comprehend. He falls
on his knees, rolls onto his back and closes his eyes.
Who will tell him where the healing starts?

v

He cries out, his body shudders
and he wakes not to one perfect answer
offered up in the blast of the west wind
but to questions that lie in the chill
of his bones, the roar of his herd,
the constant hum of the city in the valley.
Releasing his grip on this earth,
he rises to return home across the hill,
the light already failing.

A Time for Giving

Unde homines nati, durum genus.
Virgil

A Time for Giving

In the space of a month
        from mid-September

one hundred milk cows offer up
        their own to the farm

calves carried all summer
        in ribbed coracles

to be born in the reeds by the burn
        or in the lee of a dense hedge.

Each to stagger its first steps
        in the wind and rain

calling out for its mother
        and her thick yellow milk

to bond further
        with nudge and nuzzle

not knowing
        the separation to come

every heifer
        a gift for the herd

every bull
        a present for the hounds.

Annual Meadow

Blow

How often fate chooses the best of the herd to fail
so that morning he is on the phone to the practice
hoping his description alone will provide a diagnosis
and a cure without the costliness of a consultation.

The growth looks like the bubbles in new milk froth.
No, more like the dark reddish lump of haematite
I've seen in a display cabinet at the village museum.
That's not right either, doesn't capture the extent of it.

He reaches to make it real, remembers the vet's last visit:
Count Basie's big band blasting out from his battered Austin.
Picture Dizzy's puffed up cheeks as his lips are pressed hard
to the mouthpiece of the horn – the swelling's exactly that.

Trace

The journey that began
long before
a mouthful of blisters,
a shiver
a limp
carries on
beyond the barriers
of disinfectant and straw
to a hillside
where machines of disposal
shovel and stack
the rigid frames
of the bloated. Eight
hundred animals,
five-deep, doused,
torched on beds of timber,
the farmer's silhouette
lost against the flames.
Carcasses crackling on the pyre
will fill his nights
with lifeless stares.
Burn them until nothing remains.
All that is left in the morning
is the lingering stench,
the ash trace of the herd
on the snow;
the fear
that cowers downwind.

Uses

A butcher
in the back garden

finishing off his beer
boasts of wars fought,

before slitting the throat
of our old boar:

blood gushing into a pail
below blue skies.

Useful animal, the pig
It gives us thick cut ham
succulent sausages,
rashers of bacon

his words sizzle in the heat

blood for black pudding
bristles for brushes
leather for saddles,
and footballs and bags
Yes – you can find a use
for every part of the pig

except the squeal.

After the bleeding,
the scaldering,
the butchering,

it's the squeal
        that stays
piercing my summers.

The Big Mistake

The shepherd on the train told me
is to clip milking ewes too soon.

I put my newspaper down;
he'd got my attention.

Nothing puts the milk off them quicker
than a day like last Wednesday.
And when it goes off at this time of year,
it never comes back.

His warning continued

They never get so rough in the backend,
and have less protection
against the storms and winter chill.

He glanced up
to his crook in the luggage rack.

And another thing
is that the wool neither weighs so heavy
nor looks so well. It's new growth
that brings down the scales.
A fleece from a ewe that's near
hasn't the same feel as one from a ewe
that has plenty of rise and a good strong stoan.
In the beginning of July the new wool on a thin ewe
will grow more in one week under the fleece
than it will do in three with the fleece clipped off.

He summarised his argument for me:
Experienced flock-masters never clip hill stocks
before the second week of July;
in terms of the sheep's sufferings
a strong sun is little less severe than a cold rain.

Tall Fescue

He stopped there,
looked out of the window at the passing fields,
then fell asleep to Waverley
content that a stranger in a suit
had listened to his wisdom.
This wisdom I now share with you.

Cowpit Yowe

Swollen heavy with lambs,
as wide as she is long
stranded on her back
in a marshy hollow
in Hogmanay's
diminishing light.
Legs thin as kindling
signal a struggle
that slows in the sleet.
Crows spot her fleece.

So I jump the fence
cross the stranger's field
grip the tug of coarse wool
right her into a shake,
watch her stiff walk
back across the scarp,
and ponder the effort needed
to roll over the death
of one old year
into the birth of a new.

Timothy

Queen of the Sheep

The Queen of the Sheep lies in state
on a small hummock,
in the open air,
through the hottest day of the year.

No long illness,
no special message,
no official announcement,
she just rolled over and died
like many of her kind before:
a pure bred Texel. Bloodlines
don't matter
when you're gone.

Laid out in buzzing robes,
inane grin of rotten teeth,
thick rubber tongue.
Black feathered courtiers
bow to her eye sockets.
Her own incense is a rank royal odour.
Death in this heat rules the senses.

Trailing a cortege of flies and crows,
I drag the bloated corpse to the gate
by her small insubstantial legs:
a less than dignified exit.
My cheeks are tracked by sweat not tears.

The followers refuse to rise in the heat,
sit around uninterested;
there's always another.
The Queen of the Sheep is dead.
Long live the Queen.

The Daughters of Proetus

'Begin, my Muses, begin again the herdsman's song' –Thyrsis
'Don't send me any more cow poems' –Sally Evans (Poetry Scotland)

How can I possibly stop now?
My muse will not let me,
For milk is my wine.
So I'll bow down drunk again
At the shrines of bucolic beauty:
Show-day daughters of Proetus
With clippered top lines
And tail perm perfections
Parading pride as the prize.
Through a June heat haze
Gaze on graceful manicured hooves,
Haltered heads and red rosettes.
Haughty heifers of Holstein
Hold high your gleaming muzzles,
Stretch necks to graze the sky.
Bovine goddesses of milk
Shiny hides silken and pied
Swinging those glorious udders.
Oh, princesses of talcum powder
Your black has never been so dark,
Your white has never been so bright.
Our ladies of the long lactation,
Succours of this once great nation,
Accept again my humble praise.

My Wife Becomes a Field

It started in bed
a couple of new shoots sprouting from her navel;
something fungal, best not to mention,
but it spread so quickly
down her thighs along her arms,
transforming her back into a turfed lawn.
It tickles, she laughs, puts down her book.
In her meadowsweet breath
she boasts of deep roots, broad leaved foliage
shows off a greening body:
a new outfit of rampant vegetation,
but I'm no gardener, and anyway
you can't take a set of shears to your wife.
I chew on a blade of fescue,
explore the rolling hills of her breasts,
hedges form along each rib;
fingers blossom from branches into trees.
Gathering up her hair in handfuls of clover,
I gaze below tufted flower beds to each iris:
a cluster of harebells dancing.
Blowing on her neck
I launch a million dandelion clocks
across fertile valleys.
In an hour she takes our bed
from Winter to full blown Summer,
disappearing under her own pasture.
Through head high grass I follow,
falling and reaching out for warm earth.
Beneath my nails seeds germinate and grow.

Wild Poppies

A ragged band of troubadours
performs each year at this roadside venue
by the steps to the drying green.

With a burlesque rush of blood,
Spring catapults into untamed Summer,
tissues explode from a magician's fist.

Whirling arched and bowed
thin stemmed gypsies
struggle under heavy red taffeta.

Locally they dance nowhere else
bar this rough bank
among coarse grass and dockens.

Held with dependable pegs,
the dull patched workday clothes
flap applause for the dirt-verge dervishes.

Green-leaved admirers hold hands up in awe;
others buzz round the skirts' dark centres
eager with exotic notions.

Unfettered sways of Romany
plucked from the show
succumb in a sudden fall of petals.

Oh Sweet Sweet Silage

It is now that I will speak of it
a sparkling critique of it
the covered-up mystique of it
the flavour so unique of it
the strong and cocky cheek of it
the farmers' hands they reek of it
it stays with them for weeks of it
their wives they have to sleep with it
the heifers they would leap for it
with a missionary zeal for it
the all-day steaming meal of it
the sleek and textured feel of it
the polythene thin seal of it
the language forming spiel of it
the hunger storming beat of it
the winter warming heat of it
the chance to overeat of it
the ritual repeat of it
the scientific feat of it
the engineering skill of it
the building up a hill of it
the thrilling pleasing oooh of it
the spilling squeezing spew of it
the bovine teasing brew of it
the taste bud puzzle stew of it
the snappy guzzle chew of it
the happy muzzles moo of it
the love fermenting woo of it
the lovely smelly shoots of it
the swollen belly fruits of it
I fill my welly boots with it
the gorgeous pungent juice of it
my words are so effuse on it
the wonderful excuse of it
the everlasting use of it

all veggies could have fun with it
hell they could eat a ton of it
and still be never done with it
the stunning luscious vein of it
the summer sun and rain of it
the there forever stain of it
the seeping down the drain of it
the milk production gain of it
the Friesians that are fed on it
the gaudy green and red of it
I'd even make my bed in it
enjoy the sweet caress of it
and not think any less of it
the sharing out success of it
the feast for any guest of it
the old cows get the best of it
the young beasts eat the rest of it
the fabulous bequest of it
the treasured full blown breath of it
the rising after death of it
sweet resurrection of grass.

Kalashnikov's Mower

'I would have preferred to have invented something which helps people.
A lawn mower for example' –Mikhail Kalashnikov

Later you will boast
of the prototype
to the neighbour,
who leans over the fence
a witness.

Wheeling it from the shed
point out features of note –
drive shaft, half pulley, gear case,
blade cover, recoil assembly,
the gas return tube above the barrel –
all made from materials
just lying around. It is amazing
what can be done
with thought.

You comment on its accuracy, the reek
of petrol and cut grass
mown down in swathes, but not

the flutter you felt
as you flicked off the catch.

Picking Up the Song (in a Break in the Harvest)

A couple lie on a rough working coat and pluck
overripe brambles from the hedge.
Juice stained fingers reach out to grasp
their turn of an old moothie:

releasing a melody to the breeze,
mentor's refrain – echoed response,
stacking up the notes of a song
that blinds them with its silver.

In small honeycombed hollows
purple tongues search eagerly
for each other's sweet breaths,
sharing the secrets of sook and blow.

But this isn't about them,
the couple in the stubble field,
his sweat drenched shirt
beaded in barley grains and chaff,

her promises revealed
in the lightness of a summer dress;
nor the beat of their reed breathing,
lips pushed hard against hot metal,

nor even the stroking of the palms
that slowly pass back and forward
a harmonica packed with seeds.
It's simply about playing that tune.

Laidlaw

They say that some just end up bad
as though that should suffice for this:
the eldest of the brood, a black angus
fed from childhood on festering bales;
a mad beast uneasy in enclosed spaces,
heavy with dung, each breath a wound.
His wide-eyed stare a barley field on fire;
his muscled haunches thunder the night.
Circling the air with butt and bellow
his anvil thick skull puts out the stars.

~

Her slow brother came to visit one day,
followed a trail of red spots into the house
found the buckled belt, her sobbing body
a bloodied shield trampled into the carpet
uncovered beneath her a shaking son
offering up his stolen egg unbroken.

~

He charged them but was downed with a shovel.
Her brothers dragged him roaring to the pen.
They took castrators and pulled out his tongue;
in the end left him chained, neutered and mute.
Across the sharp stubble of harvest fields
the family carried their sister home.

Stack

Far from the breezy freedom of stubbled fields
we were the reluctant prisoners of the big shed.

Left behind to put away safe the stringed harvest
our short wordless journeys to lift and stack, back
to front, until bales were jammed against the roof,
careful not to choke the elevator's incessant feed.
All day, tractors and trailers arrived in the steading
high loads swaying round the final tight corner
with the unsteady grace of an uncle returned
from the dancing: serenading stars, fou as a puggie.

No less musical the relentless putt putt judder
of an old elevator, black smoke signalling its effort
the stiff lever cranking up the angle of ascent
the conveyer's ribbed belt struggling to send up
single file blocks of hay to be caught at the top
by coarse-handed inmates of that shrinking space,
bare backs hunched inches from the tin's hot girdle,
a sauna stinging eyes blood red with salted sweat.

Raw fingers gripping twine sensed their weight
and shape, and knew the perfect fit of bale to bale
that would interlock, secure that covered stack
until winter when each in turn would be released
returned to the very fields that first offered them up
broken open like bread on the now barren ground
sustaining the rough-haired heifers until the thaw.

Black Cart

'Time's wagon ever-onward driven' –Alexander Pushkin

The stook building had finished early that day
so all of us jumped a lift on the miller's big cart
discarding thin shirts in a pile behind the driver.

Harvest's favourite sons bronzed and bawdy,
we stood at the back shouting on passers by,
toasting our handiwork with sickly warm beer.

Under a big sky, Johnny sang something coarse
and we bellowed along proud of our own voices,
confident of tomorrows, as if we owned the sun.

Some cursing an old Clydesdale's slow rhythm
raced ahead of the cart impatient for the ceilidh
while others stayed on through a sunset's glow.

Beyond Harelaw the mare laboured on the brae,
strained on its breast strap; the dray shuddered
and empty bottles rolled across its wooden floor,

boards stained with the dry blood of dead beasts.
We crouched down quick, clung on to the sides,
felt then a first shiver and reached for our shirts.

Passing those unmarked crossings and road ends,
the horse slowed on its journey but never stopped
so Johnny, his song long silent, must've slipped off

unnoticed, and the others too when their time came,
like orchards' ripe fruit, dropped soft to the ground,
disappeared fast down dirt tracks and narrow lanes.

Crested Hair

Those of us that remained pulled our knees up tight,
our thin joints stiffening in the moonlit glint of sickle,
our whispers drifting away on a winnowing breeze.

Storm clouds rolled in to snuff out every dead star
until there was just me huddled by the driver's back
the darkest mile left to go and too late for the dance.

Crested Hair

The Progressive Canadian Barn Dance

The first time she wore the new dress
was at the farmers' harvest dance
on a night breathless and warm.

Uneasy with her body's new bloom
she would have sat the night out
had her mother not dragged her up

to be thrown around like a doll
from rough hands to rough hands,
from Anderson to Macgregor

from Macgregor to young Wilson
in his father's tight tweed jacket,
from Wilson to club foot Brogan

from club foot Brogan to Lamberton
in his scabby working bunnet
from Lamberton to the moleman

from the moleman to his apprentice
staring at her in his strange way,
from the apprentice to Patterson,

who danced fast but talked slow.
From Patterson to Uncle Jack
(not her real uncle of course)

who held her too close and grinned
talked about how much she'd grown up.
She struggled free from his grip

found one of the Mackenzie boys
from one of them to the other
with their shiny new market boots

and on to old Wilson with his crook
and on to his buddy Baxter
smelling of his black face flock;

from his strong stench to Anderson
scratching his ringworm;
from Anderson to Macgregor

who birled her until she was dizzy;
from Macgregor to young Wilson
(they say he'll never be his father)

from Wilson to Brogan's brown eyes,
from brown-eyed Brogan to Lamberton
who threw his bunnet onto a seat.

She grabbed him. The pace quickened,
the dance lifting her dress up light as air,
she spun him away before moving on

from Lamberton to the moleman
sweating lochs through his winter shirt.
After the moleman his apprentice;

from the cross-eyed apprentice
to big Patterson flustered and red.
From Patterson on not to Uncle Jack

who was wheezing at the bar
but the clumsy Mackenzie boys
taking turns to bruise her feet

Creeping Bent

before passing her to old Wilson
who staggered to keep up with her,
mentioned he once courted her mother –

Oh surely not she laughed out loud,
winked at him in a new confidence,
glanced back at her mother

then on to his drinking pal Baxter.
From his beery breath to Anderson
from Anderson to Macgregor

from Macgregor to young Wilson
from Wilson to Johnny Brogan
who clasped her hand tight, echoed

her smile and the music stopped.

McLean's Way Home

Famed for his love of Laphroaig,
a 1957 gold Fergie,
and most of all his homing instinct, his exits
from local barn dances were legend. Refusing lifts
when the time was right
he would take off as the crow flies
straight across fields over ditches and dykes
dancing with shadows on the hill.
On longer journeys he would nap under hedges,
rise with bird call and early light.

One morning his wife found him
snoring on his back in the spare room
sprouting hay like a scarecrow.
Around the same time
Andy from Dampton farm
discovered his field of scattered bales
assembled in neat stacks.
Like the signature stench of fox
they marked someone passing through,
a day's work already done.

Marsh Fox-tail

The Balemartin Bard

He could be gone for days

moving between the ceilidh houses
of neighbouring townships.

Even in his absence
they came to the croft,

the daughters and sons of cottars,
appearing in ones and twos

from the long grass of the machair,
ragged and hungry for new words.

Leaving the chores
his sister welcomed them all.

Her rough hands would point
below the broken lintel

to the driftwood door
where he'd carelessly scribbled

his most recent bàrdachd.
She would read it to them

as slowly as the tides turn
letting the music of each line

fill their ears.
In the singing voices

that departed across the fields
she would listen

for the echo of her brother.

White Beak-sedge

Griot

for Toumani Diabaté

He followed the rumour of himself
along the length of our sad valley

to arrive that night at our barn
with every local farmer packed inside.

Because he could see our hunger
he sat astride a cow hide gourd

sprouting a spine, a spreading fan,
half lute, half harp and started to play.

His hands darted across its strings
fingers and thumbs weaving

seasons with their rise and fall,
summer breeze and river spate.

As night became day
he sang of cicada and baobab

failed harvests and disease
and we listened and knew ourselves

a little better, and so followed his words
from barn to barn, field to field,

through days and weeks and months.
In time this pilgrim became our witness

his music became our lands,
our story his song.

Meadow Fescue

Inheritance

Sequiturque patrem non passibus aequis.

Virgil

Not Exactly Ships in the Night

Not exactly ships, father,
that is not the nature of our paths
crossing on the steep slope of Horsewood Road
though sometimes it rains so hard, so long
I feel the River Gryffe could rise up to meet us,
carry us off across submerged fields.

No boatman, I wear a suit, walk
on worn soles that let in water
and you travel in that rusted Skoda
spluttering through its first climb of the day;
struggling as we do with the early starts:
the first bus, to a desk in a distant city;
the first cow, eager to be fed and milked.

Nor is it night, though few in this village
have risen yet to call this darkness morning –
they miss those moments of our passing,
a blast of the horn, a headlight flash, a wave,
sometimes a window rolled down:
Get to work
        Aye you too
and always your smile
staking its claim, remaining bright
in the ebb of streetlights, stars.

Meikle Burntshields

Lost

Lolling tongues are for dogs,
not the boy sprawled flat on his back
in the barn, out of his mind.
        He'd have kicked him
there and then,
taught him a lesson like he did
the collies that strayed
but for that look in his son's eyes.

Siblings

i. brothers

Two brothers trapped in harness
working their barren years.
Close enough to share a shadow
they've never known the blessed
relief of days apart.

A life sentence of love
poured out on the beasts alone
leaves nothing for kin;
a bleak legacy for those unwilling
to share this small kingdom.

Outliving becomes the only goal,
watching the other stoop and fail.
Mistrust is the tie that silence binds
tightening like a ring on a lamb's tail
till it severs and falls from life itself.

ii. sisters

Bent by seasons on the hill
their heads drawn to the land
in days of laboured prayer

they share their shape, their walk,
their whispered talk,
their calling in the yowes,

the shedding, shearing, dipping,
their daily porridge,
their patched-up working frocks,

the landscape of each face
stained an earth-dirt tan
etched with a furrowed burden.

Widowhood brought them back
to work the family land
accepting the inheritance:

the draughty farmhouse
and now with failing limbs
their parents' ground floor bed.

Even to share with their last breath
the family grave their father bought
to keep his loved ones near.

A tie many would rail against,
but love also in the bond
that would unravel if one should go

Shillingworth

but this is only idle chat:
the day won't stop, with jobs to do
the sisters are already up and out.

Silence

In a small kitchen
they sit for breakfast;
silence seasons their porridge

Though he reads in the paper
of falling market prices
he says nothing

Though he leaves his food,
pushes the plate away
she says nothing

Though winter-feed stocks dwindle,
and animals sicken
he says nothing

Though too often he burns his soul
in cheap whisky
she says nothing

Though he wakes in the dark
carcass pyres in his eyes
he says nothing

Though last night beyond the whins
she buried his old shot-gun
she says nothing.

Mid Barnaigh

Still Life

She lay dead in the early morning dew
in a working man's bunnet, worn wellies,

wrapped in a shapeless woollen jumper:
its ragged sleeves soaking wet and sticky

from the many mouths of suckling calves;
her small frame cruciform, hands reaching out

for the two black plastic pails of milk
like large eyes creamy with glaucoma;

both set carefully down as she fell
so as not to spill one drop of the feed.

East Barnaigh

Not Missing Michael Jackson
Jimmy Baxter (1921–2009)

Three days after that other funeral
we sat together on hard pews
to celebrate the life
of a man who knew who he was,
who worked the land from birth to death
and put no burden on us
to see him as anything more,
so we were happy to sing for him
All things bright and beautiful –
to let that be our farewell.

For a couple of minutes, no more,
the minister talked of the man himself,
a slow but imprecise driver
whose old and battered pick up
gathered dents and paint-flecks,
scratches like keepsakes,
from all his neighbours' farms.
We were there to bury a modest man,
the sun streaming through stained glass.

Laigh Auchencloich

The Funeral for John of Kirkton

Ancient farmers with sticks
hirple up
the narrow road
to the hill-top cemetery;
one more procession
in a Summer of black harvests.
Even in this August light
they're fading before my eyes.

My father delivers the eulogy –
heartfelt, emotional.
Seventy years of long days,
diminishing returns.
Family man, stockman,
man of the soil.
The land his life.
He finishes abruptly,
looks at me.
We both know
he's talking about himself.

High Auchencloich

Progress

Same year as that photograph of the man
who stopped the tanks' progress in the square
my father strikes a similar pose, facing up
to a new red and black Case International.

Dwarfed by the advances he supported
in his lifetime, he's seen the work pass
from Clydesdale and Shire to diesel breeds,
his horseman father becoming mechanic.

No stand-off this, but simply a witness
to the present, an acceptance of a future
where in the shadow of giant tractors
he will wilt back into the ground.

Laigh Auchensale

Clearing Out the Cow Shed

At five a.m. a cold carcass awaits.
In the darkness of the shed I pick out
the rictus curve of rusted mudguard,

climb into the seat, hard, unforgiving,
the plastic steering wheel as stiff
as the ageing hands that grip it.

I turn the key to the right one stop;
the sick yellow eye winks back.
With diminishing faith I turn it over

and over, until, with a Lazarus shudder,
it belches out black smoke.
I stamp on the clutch, ram the stick forward,

find one of the gears that actually works;
and we are off up and down the rows,
clearing the slurry from last night's cattle.

My senses struggle to wake to the chore –
that jerky descent of scraper to concrete.
When its lights fail, I'm left to navigate blind,

in part through the half-remembered,
in part through my clumsy reflex to the rub
of the big wheels on the edge of the grip.

I crawl the narrow aisle between cubicles
all the time dragging the shit behind me,
finding my hesitant way to the end.

The Braes

Old Collie

While milking together
my father shouts across the parlour
an idea for my next poem:

How about a working collie –
one that's on its last legs.
I tell him it has been done before.

Unwilling to chase this sentimental stick,
I leave it well alone,
turn away, but feel it lying there

becoming hair and bone
crouching low, resting its arthritic frame,
flecked muzzle flat on its front paws.

Lifting itself slowly to its feet
it sniffs out the few short steps to my father,
where we both knew it was bound to go.

Clochoderick Stone

Because I no longer have the words
to soothe away your lot my brother
the run of bad luck, and now your dog

I offer you a stone, no precious gem
for your ring finger, shined to a sparkle,
it would too soon be lost in the slurry

but instead a boulder dumped in a field
a couple of miles from Kilbarchan Cross.
A dull volcanic twice the height of man,

it has a cracked rough lustre of journey –
thousands of years ago the last ice age
dragged it here all the way from Argyll.

Legend has it discarded from a giant's boot,
a site of a king's magician's summons
to the gods for victory in the next battle

and a rocking stone for dispensing justice.
If only that were the case for you today.
It does not move now so you must go to it.

Stand close and touch this way marker;
listen closely to what it is telling you:
Even the longest winters have an end.

Lawmarnock

Whin Field
James McConnell (1905–2000)

It's Jimmy, faither.
It's Jimmy, Margaret's son come to see you.
This is my last visit.
You nod in my direction,
a brief recognition in the fog.
Words are beyond you.

The doctor says breathe in, faither.
Don't cough.
Your wife scolds gently,
always the nurse, always
there. Your children
take turns to sit with you,
to sleep beside you at night
as they did in the beginning.

Towering over my childhood
with the strength of a heavy horse,
you would work fields and gardens
from dawn to dusk.

Weeks before,
with your colour
draining into the sheets,
I reached out,
lifted up the lightness of your brittle frame,
carried you to the wheelchair. Outside

there was nowhere you didn't want to go, checking
every byre and cubicle house,
the lambs in the bottom field,
making whispered comments, missing
nothing. Then out beyond

Barnbrock

the hay shed
that would burn down so soon after.
They never told you,
closing your curtains;
fire engines drove by silent.

At the silage pit we stopped
again. Looking at the hillside,
you talked of the battle
to clear the whins,
pointed to an explosion of spines.
I warned George:
don't let them grow back in.

Hard Rind – Love of This Kind
Barbara McConnell (1912–2008)

i. If my gran had ever met Don Giovanni

If my gran had ever met Don Giovanni
she would've got the measure of the man:
shown him her strong faith, stout resolve,
gripping her bible as tight as a lover's hand,

not succumbing to his sly and easy charm
as he whistled carefree by the byre door
setting himself as a lure in his own trap,
belly full of stolen fruits from her garden.

Her scowl was death sitting at your table.
You'll have had your tea then, my lord.
She'd utter just one line. Its full stop
would be a barrel closing click at his back.

ii. the kiss

I watched my grandparents shrink
into the worn chairs
of their tiny living room,
inhabit confused conversations:
arguments of gruff deafness.

My grandmother called him *faither*
though she chided him as a bairn.
A haystack, he stood firm
against her autumnal blasts:
turned up the TV sound.

Their many tender moments
were rarely shared with others
and had to be caught in mirrors,
stolen with a sideways glance
so I treasure this one most of all:

She placed her arthritic hand on his,
whispered to him like a young lover,
then under their cottage's low roof
left the softest kiss on his cheek
as he lay there three days dead.

iii. marmalade

My first surprise was that
the recipe you recited
from your hospital bed

was not yours
but your mother's mother's:
Granny Brown's golden hoard.

The second surprise –
this gift I took for granted,
jam jars filled in an instant –

takes three full days to make
and only in the brief season
of bitter blood red oranges.

A recipe measured
in tumblers and pounds:
one lemon, oranges quartered,

pips removed; left in water,
the fruit minced, steeped
for twenty four hours.

A cycle of boiling
and leaving to settle
patience repeated because

love of this kind
takes time to produce
the tart and the sweet

that stirred my tongue
the soft jelly, the hard rind
the amber sun

that lit up my breakfast,
my kitchen shelf,
my memory still.

Lawmarnock Wood in Autumn

You, who never asked for anything
now and again would mention
how much you loved
that view across the valley,
We talked of photographs,
paintings – a framed gift for you.

Now it's too late to capture
what you loved most,
the wood's slow turning,
those moments before leaf fall,
the way it lifts clear of early mist
from the banks of the Locher burn
to hug the contours of two hills.

The skyline of your working days, a vocal
tapestry of russets and yellows,
a gathering of old friends after the harvest.
You'd watch and listen
to the sway of their dancing
as the last of the berries
were picked from the hedgerows.

Scents of change
in a strengthening breeze, in the stiff
ache of your joints;
that growing taste of damp
you treasured for its burnished afterglow,
offering up both bird chorus and lonely owl,
celebration and melancholy.

Mother, this is January.
I cannot give you again
Lawmarnock Wood in Autumn.

Monkland

Mother Harvest
Margaret Carruth (1938–2008)

Mother forgive me these last visits.
Before it is too late, I have come

to support again your painful shuffle as if
barefoot over a stubble field;

to harvest your every smile, your love
for others, your hope for all

our futures, to gather in each precious word,
stack more carefully in my heart-barn

your deep tone of casual conversation.
Seed your half-forgotten memories in mine: the child

sprouting from Ayrshire clay; the adult
working the seasons on the hill.

All these and more I must reap to feed
the hunger in my remaining winters.

These rushed short days with you
bringing in the bales before the rain.

Dampton

Conversing with Angels

Recently you've glimpsed them more
often on quiet roads to your son's farm
through the black mornings before dawn.

Your headlamps launch these night guardians
from flashes of eyes and ruffled feathers
into silent prophets of white-winged flight.

Last night you stood on the cottage doorstep
at the boundary where village becomes field,
offered up a wordless invocation to the stars.

A messenger high in the old bell tower
delivered an answer, unearthly and hoarse,
as many have done throughout your life.

You replied and another joined in
echoing from a small congregation of oak;
a third spoke up from beyond the river.

Today you recount those conversations:
a voice reaffirming its connection to the unseen;
and a faith that calls out confident of response.

Barnbeth

Leaking Bucket

The argument for an honest wage was lost.
You could not face the once-and-for-all,
so sent down the farm's potholed track
three of your cows each market day.

A leaking away as though from a holed pail
with its drip, drip, drip of milk
to the ground, cheaper than bottled water,
more painful than a long prayer in blood. As if

each small float load of cattle
was a shiny white pebble dropped by you
to follow back home in the moonlight,
a faint path to a place no longer there.

Botherickfield

84

Farm Sale

Everything is numbered and must go
so he sits at the back of the shed
while the crowd pick over the final lots.

He lays his cap flat on his knee, and slowly
stretches a stiff finger to find
the faded cross hatch flecks

tracing each tweed field on his bunnet,
whispering their old names to himself,
walking the boundaries of his lost world.

Clevans

Until the Cows Come Home

First I will give you names
for names are important.
You will take my hand
and we will do nothing else
all day but dance outside
just the two of us
barefoot
Across the fields of
Meikle Burntshields
Little Burntshields
Shillingworth
Mid Barnaigh
East Barnaigh
Laigh Auchencloich
High Auchencloich
Laigh Auchensale
The Braes
not stopping
until we've covered
the quiet lands of
Law
Lawmarnock
Barnbrock
Moniabrock
Monkland
Dampton
Barnbeth
Botherickfield
Clevans
Lochend
A sombre waltz in long grass
for the lost herds of the shire.

Lochend

Inheritance

Together we stand
late in an autumn afternoon
in the doorway to the byre:
father and son looking across
the lands of High Auchensale
to the long-shadowed milkers
still grazing in the corner field
and I, the eldest, know
I've walked away from all this.

With the partial commitment
of relief milkings on Saturdays
or a help at harvest time
I've turned down the full embrace
of a life wedded to the land
as the keeper of the herd
though we will not speak of it
now or ever –
letting our silence be a sign.

For you are my father
in much more than looks
and my real inheritance
is the handing down of being,
a shared passion for
what this place means.
Neither of us live here any more,
so each return journey
is a reconnecting.

And while we are able
we'll always come back
each to be judged in turn
by what we pass on to others,
but not now as we bring in the cows
Away back,
Get away back
two voices in the failing light
calling out together.

Notes

The footers in the first section are the fields of High Auchensale our family farm. The footers in the second section are types of grasses and the footers in the third section are the local farms that have stopped dairying and sold their herds.

Daughters of Proetus – Proetus in Greek mythology was a king of Argos. He had three daughters who were driven mad either because they had insulted the goddess Hera or because they would not accept the new rites of Dionysus. They believed themselves to be cows and wandered the land, mooing.

The Big Mistake – a found poem from the wise words of Henry J Clayboddie.

Acknowledgements

I would like to thank all those who helped with shaping of this collection including Gerry Cambridge, Gerrie Fellows, Richie McCaffrey, William Bonar, Peter Mackay, Alexander Hutchison Eleanor Livingstone, Helena Nelson, Diana Hendry and Hamish Whyte.

I would like to thank the following where versions of some of the poems appeared originally:

The Red Wheelbarrow, Black Mountain Review, The Dark Horse, Drey, The Eildon Tree, Envoi, Gutter, Herald, New Writing Scotland (20, 22, 23, 24, 25, 28, 29, 30), *Northwords, Poetry Scotland,* The Scottish Poetry Library, *Scotsman* and previous publications in Mariscat and Happenstance press.

Poems included were also prize winners in Edinburgh Fringe, Ragged Raven, Wigtown and William Soutar poetry competitions and have been published in a number of anthologies including *The Oxford Poets 2010, Kin, Skeins of Greece, New Boots and Pantisocries* and translated into urdu in *A Change in the Light* anthology.

Homecoming was the winner of Renfrewshire New Poets competition in 1998.

The Man Who Wanted to Hug Cows was chosen for 100 Favourite Scottish poems anthology in 2006.

The Moleman's Apprentice and *The Big Mistake* were chosen for the Best Scottish Poems in 2006 and 2007 respectively.

Educating the Farm Boy was part of my solo exhibition Cowpit Yowe held in Tramway, Glasgow in 2008.

The Word was commissioned to mark the 10th anniversary of the Aye Write Book festival in 2015.

Jim Carruth was born in 1963 in Johnstone, Renfrewshire, and grew up on his family's farm near Kilbarchan. His first chapbook collection *Bovine Pastoral* was published in 2004. He has won the James McCash poetry competition, the Callum Macdonald memorial Award and the McLellan poetry prize and was awarded a Robert Louis Stevenson Fellowship in 2009. In 2014 He was appointed Glasgow Poet Laureate. He is the co-founder and current chair of St Mungo's Mirrorball – the Glasgow poetry network and artistic adviser for the StAnza International Poetry Festival. In 2015 *Killochries* was shortlisted for the Fenton Aldeburgh first collection award and the Saltire Scottish Poetry Book of the Year and in 2016 it was shortlisted for the Seamus Heaney Centre For Poetry Prize for first full collection.

By the same author

Poetry
Migration
Killochries
Prodigal
Rider at the Crossing
Working the Hill
Grace Notes 1959
Cowpit Yowe
Baxter's Old Ram Sang the Blues
High Auchensale
Bovine Pastoral

As Editor
The Laws of the Game
Spellwinders
Lot 76